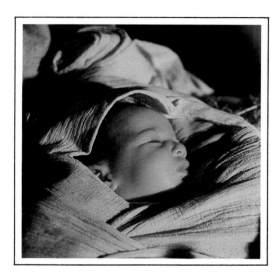

Mary Had a Baby
The Story of Christmas

The Genesis Project, Inc.
Washington, D.C.
1981

Graphic Credits

The text of this book was phototypeset in Alphatype Caledo by Harlowe Phototypography, Inc., Brentwood, Maryland. The color separations were done by The Lanman Progressive Corporation, Washington, D.C. Printing was done by Creative Printing, Inc., Hyattsville, Maryland. Binding was done by Economy Bookbinding Corporation, Kearny, New Jersey. Production and book design were directed by Ann Cherryman.

Library of Congress Catalog Card Number: 81-83203

ISBN 0-86702-048-2

Text: Evelyn Bence

Text and photographs © 1981 by The Genesis Project, Inc.

Additional copies of **Mary Had a Baby: The Story of Christmas** can be ordered from The Genesis Project, Inc. P.O. Box 37282, Washington, D.C. 20013, or by calling (800) 336-4545.

Mary Had a Baby

When King Herod ruled Judea, there lived a righteous couple who had no children. For years Zechariah, a Jewish priest, and his wife Elizabeth had prayed for a baby, but they had given up hope that their prayers would ever be answered.

One day Zechariah was chosen to burn incense on the altar of the Lord. While he was alone inside the temple, the angel Gabriel appeared. Zechariah was terrified, but the angel immediately said, "Don't be afraid, for I've come to tell you that you and Elizabeth will have a son. You are to call him John. He will be a holy man of God, preparing the Lord's people for his coming."

Zechariah didn't believe the message. He knew that old women never have children, so he asked the angel for proof. Gabriel gave him a sign: Zechariah couldn't speak when he opened his mouth.

The people who were waiting outside started to worry and wonder what was keeping Zechariah in the temple. Finally he appeared. Because he could not talk, but only gesture, the people knew he had seen a vision.

Zechariah soon went home to Elizabeth, and the angel's words came true. Elizabeth became pregnant.

Six months later in Galilee, north of Judea, Gabriel visited Elizabeth's relative, Mary. His message to the young woman was astonishing and puzzling. She would have a baby who would be the Son of God. "Call him Jesus," he said. "He will rule Israel forever."

Mary didn't understand how this could be, since she was a virgin. So the angel explained that God would be Jesus' father. Before Gabriel left, he told Mary about Elizabeth's baby. Mary immediately went to Judea to visit her.

When Elizabeth saw Mary, she rejoiced, for she knew that Mary's baby would be special. Elizabeth blessed her for believing the angel's words. Mary, filled with joy, praised God for blessing Israel through her. After staying with Elizabeth about three months, Mary returned to her home at Nazareth in Galilee.

Elizabeth delivered a son, as the angel had promised. The neighbors assumed that the boy would be named Zechariah, after his father. But because Zechariah couldn't speak, they asked Elizabeth to name the child. "John," she said.

They didn't believe her. Then they asked Zechariah, who wrote on a tablet, "His name is John." At that instant Zechariah's voice was restored and he told the people that his son would become a great prophet.

In Nazareth, Joseph had promised to become Mary's husband. When he found out that Mary was going to have a baby, he could have chosen to have her stoned to death or he could have chosen to break their agreement quietly. Instead, he chose to marry her because an angel appeared to him in a dream to say that God was responsible for the child.

Joseph and Mary traveled to Bethlehem, Joseph's home town, because Caesar, the Roman ruler, had ordered everyone to pay a tax.

The trip was long and Mary grew tired. When the couple finally arrived in Bethlehem, there were no vacant rooms, so they stayed in a stable-cave.

There Mary gave birth to Jesus. She wrapped him in clean cloths and put him in a manger.

That night an angel appeared to shepherds who were watching their sheep in the fields outside Bethlehem. The men were terrified. The angel's first words were, "Don't be afraid! I bring you good news. Today the Saviour, Christ the Lord, was born in Bethlehem."

God's messenger told them how to recognize Jesus: by the cloths and the manger. And then a host of angels appeared and sang praises to God, offering peace to earth. When the angels disappeared, the shepherds hurried to town where they found Mary, Joseph, and the baby, just as they had been told. They repeated the angel's words. Mary thought about them and remembered them the rest of her life.

At the same time, a star appeared in the sky and shone in a country far east of Bethlehem. Men who studied the heavens saw this extraordinary star and knew it was the star of a king. They followed it westward toward Judea. When they came to Jerusalem, the capital, they asked where they could find the newly born king.

The questions of the wise men reached King Herod, who asked the teachers of the land if they knew what these foreigners could be talking about. "The prophets told of a leader who would be born in Bethlehem," they said.

Herod called the wise men to a secret meeting and told them to go find the baby. He wanted them to come back and share the good news of the birth with him, so that he could worship also. Or so he pretended.

The wise men continued to Bethlehem, found Jesus, and worshiped him by giving gifts of gold, frankincense, and myrrh.

But they did not return to Jerusalem or Herod, but went home by another route. An angel had warned the wise men in a dream that Herod had wicked plans.

Herod intended to kill Jesus as soon as the wise men told him where the infant was. He did not want anyone threatening his throne. When Herod found out that the wise men had by-passed Jerusalem, he was so angry that he killed all the baby boys two years old and under who lived in and around Bethlehem.

Jesus was saved from Herod's sword because God had sent Joseph a dream too. An angel told him to take Mary and Jesus to Egypt.

The holy family quickly started on their journey.

Mary and Joseph and Jesus stayed in Egypt until Herod had died. Then they moved back to Nazareth in Galilee, where Jesus grew "in wisdom and stature, and in favor with God and man."